779.92

Fitcher's Bird

Photography by
CINDY SHERMAN

based on a tale by
the Brothers Grimm

RIZZOLI
NEW YORK

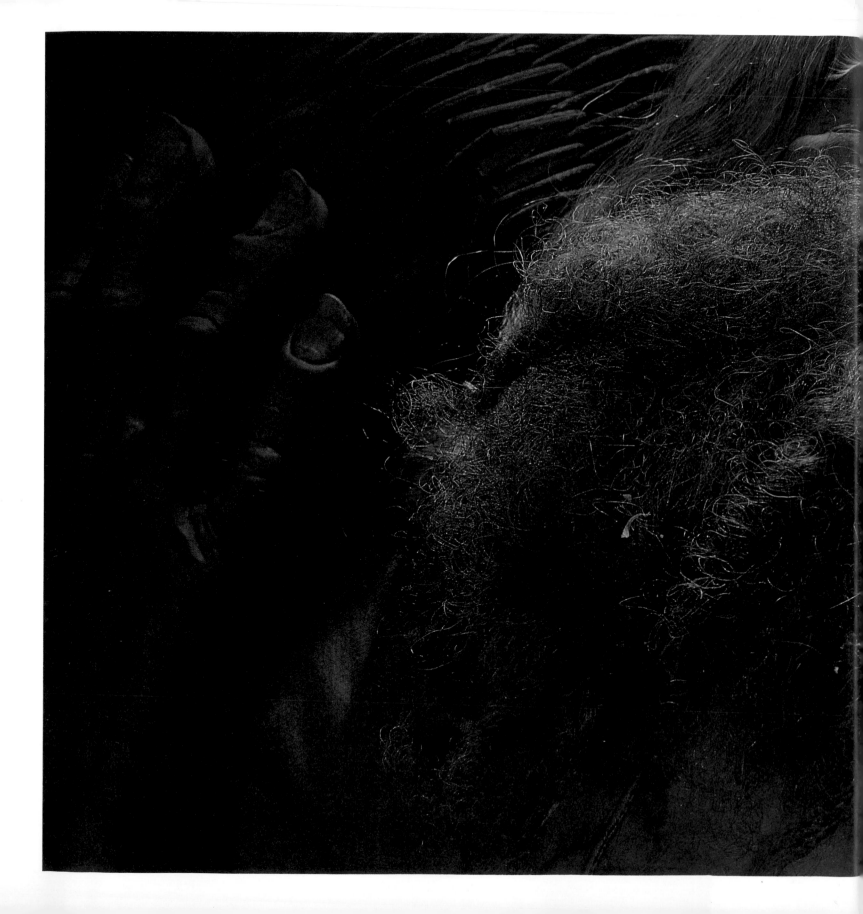

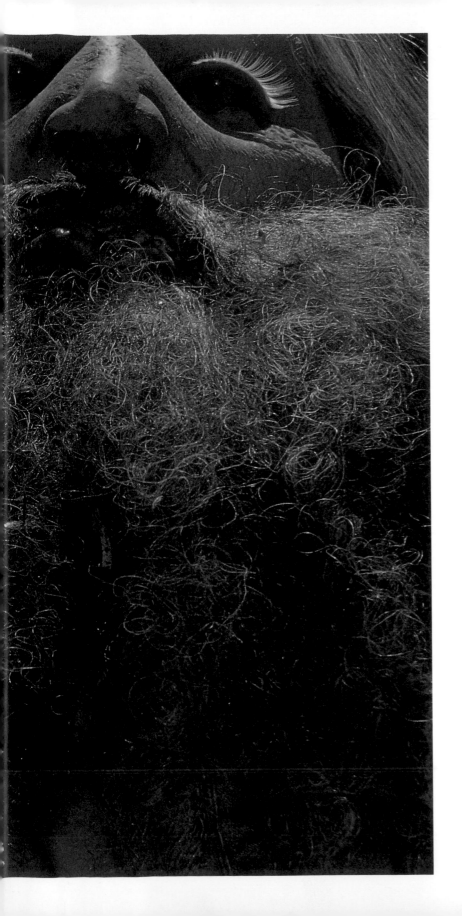

NOW THIS IS A STORY for those who are not squeamish, for it is about a wicked wizard who liked to cut people up. This wicked wizard's name was Fitcher, and he used to disguise himself as a poor man with a basket and go begging from house to house to catch beautiful girls. His power was so great that all he had to do was touch someone, and that person could not move away from him and had to do what he wanted. The spell would only be broken by a woman who proved to be obedient to his will and agree to marry him, because, of course, then no spell would be needed.

ONE DAY Fitcher went to the house of a man whom he knew had three lovely daughters. He had his basket with him.

"A crust of bread for a poor man," he cried weakly, approaching the man's door. Out came the oldest daughter with some bread. When Fitcher reached for it, he touched the maiden's hand, and she was then in his power and had to get into the basket and be carried off.

He took her to his house which stood in the middle of a dark and dismal forest filled with strange beasts that Fitcher had enchanted.

AT FIRST, Fitcher treated the maiden kindly and gave her everything she wanted. But that did not last long. Within a few days he said, "My dear, I must go away for a day or two, but you will be quite safe. Here are the keys to the house, which you are free to explore all you like. But do not go into the room whose lock fits the smallest key." Then he gave her an egg, saying, "Take this egg with you wherever you go, and be very careful with it, for you must return it to me exactly as it is in its present form."

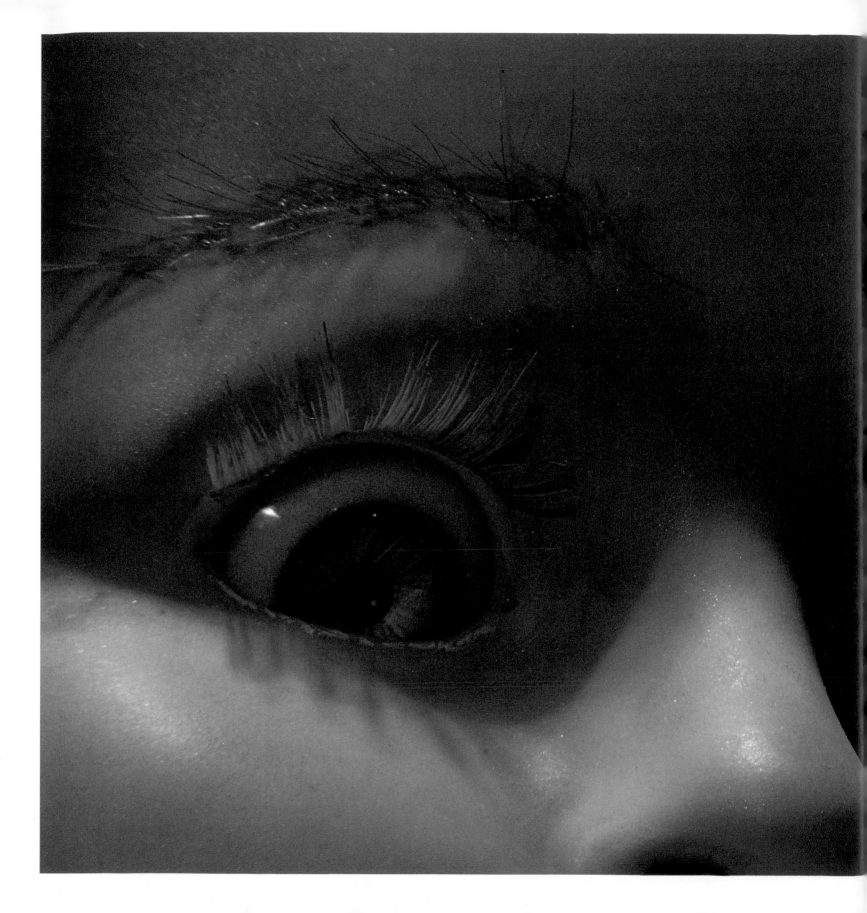

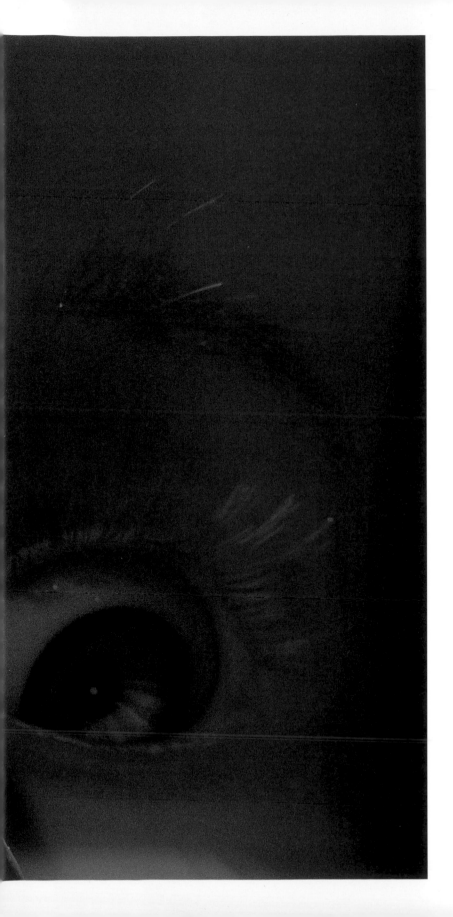

THE MAIDEN was curious, but she promised to obey Fitcher in everything he said. As soon as he was gone she began exploring, and she found many splendid things—rooms filled with gowns and shoes, silver and gold in great chests, exotic birds with colorful feathers, and bottles and jars of magic potions. Several times she passed by the door of the forbidden room, but at last she could no longer contain her curiosity and unlocked the door.

AS SOON AS she was inside, she gasped and wished that she had not gone in, for in the center of the room stood a large cauldron filled with blood and the remains of cut-up people. Next to the basin was a block of wood with a glistening axe on top of it. The maiden was so frightened that she let go of the egg which fell with a splash into the cauldron. Quickly she pulled it out and wiped off the blood—but the blood appeared again immediately, and no matter how she washed it, she could not remove the stains.

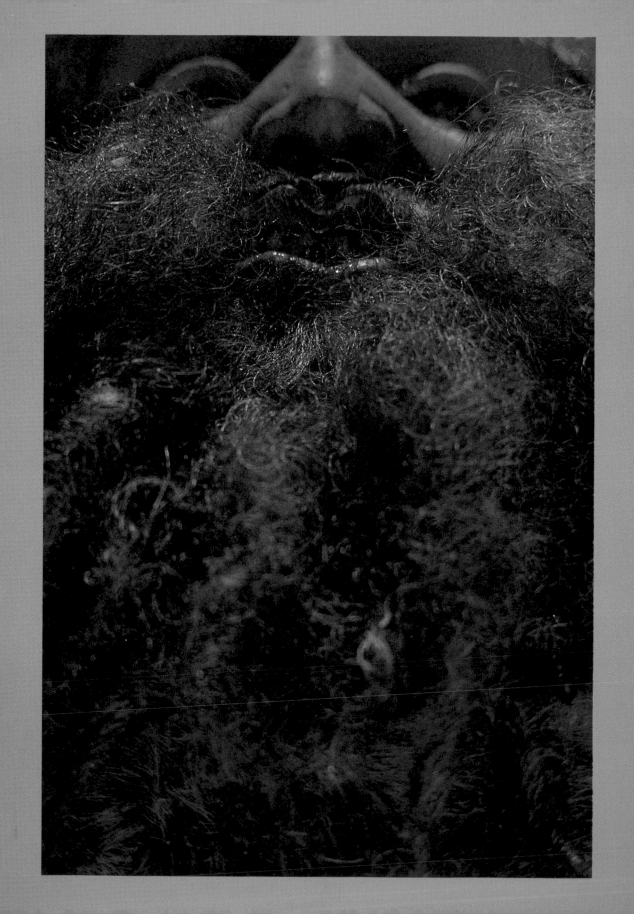

WHEN Fitcher returned, he greeted the maiden and said, "Now where are my keys and where is the egg?"

"Here they are," she said, handing him the keys first and then, trembling, the egg.

When he saw the blood on the egg, he knew she had disobeyed him. He threw her down, dragged her along by her hair, cut her head off on the block, and chopped her into pieces, so that her blood flowed on the floor. Then he tossed her into the basin with the others.

Then he set off for the same house again.

"A CRUST OF BREAD for a poor man," he cried in a piteous voice, and soon the second daughter came out with a piece of bread. He touched her as he had touched her sister, and in a flash was carrying her off to his house in the woods. All happened as before, and soon Fitcher went off again with his basket, this time to fetch the third and youngest sister.

The youngest sister was also the cleverest, and she was already suspicious of Fitcher. Again, all happened as before: Fitcher carried her away in his basket, treated her kindly at first, and then, in a few days, told her he must go away. He gave her the keys and the egg, and instructed her as he had instructed her sisters.

As soon as he left, this maiden first put the egg in a box lined with goose down to keep it safe.

*T*HEN with great care, she explored the house, and came at last to the forbidden room. Like her sisters, she went in, and cried when she saw what was in the cauldron. But keeping her wits about her, she set about gathering the parts of her sisters together. Soon she had laid all the pieces out in their proper order: head, body, arms, and legs. When nothing more was missing, the pieces began to move and join until they were whole. The two maidens then assisted their sister in helping the other poor victims in the cauldron, who thanked them joyfully many times over and then fled to their homes.

BUT the sisters stayed behind and whispered together, making plans. Then the youngest hid the other two in a little room Fitcher rarely used.

Fitcher returned soon after and demanded, "Where are my keys and my egg?" She brought him both, and the egg was white and unstained.

"My dear," he said after he examined it, "you have passed the test all others have failed; you shall be my bride."

This did not please the maiden, but she pretended it did, and agreed, for then she knew Fitcher would no longer have power over her, and would do everything she wished.

"Before I can marry you," she said, "you must share your gold with my poor mother and father; I shall put some in a basket for you to carry to them on your back. While you are gone, I will get ready."

FITCHER was not pleased with parting with his treasure, but knew he had to agree. The maiden, saying she would fill the basket, went to where she had hidden her sisters and said, "Quickly climb into this basket, and he will carry you home—but remember, as soon as you arrive, send our father and all our cousins to save me."

The older girls climbed into the basket, and their younger sister then covered them carefully with gold. Then she called Fitcher and, showing him the basket, said, "You must carry this to my father's house—but do not stop along the way, not even to rest. I shall be watching you through my little window and if you stop I will know."

*T*HE WIZARD lifted the basket onto his back, and carried it away, but it was heavy. After a while, he felt he could go no further, so he sat down. But before he had eased the basket from his shoulders, the oldest sister cried, "What, Fitcher, didn't I tell you not to rest? I can see you through my little window; go on your way!"

FITCHER thought it was his bride-to-be who spoke, and, as he wished to please her, he stood up again and walked on. Thus, every time he wanted to rest, one or the other sister ordered him on. So in awhile, exhausted, he stumbled into the parents' house, and dropped the basket on the floor. Then, gasping, he sank down to rest—the sweat pouring off his face. While his back was turned, the two girls crept out of the basket and spoke to their father and sent for their cousins.

MEANWHILE, the youngest sister took a skull that Fitcher, being a wizard, used as an ornament, and decked it with flowers and jewels so that from a distance, it would look like a living person.

On the day she expected Fitcher to return, the bride-to-be poured honey all over herself, and then she cut open a feather bed and rolled in the feathers until she looked like a feathered creature herself—like one of Fitcher's strange birds. Then she hopped down the path leading from the house, bobbing her head and holding her arms like wings.

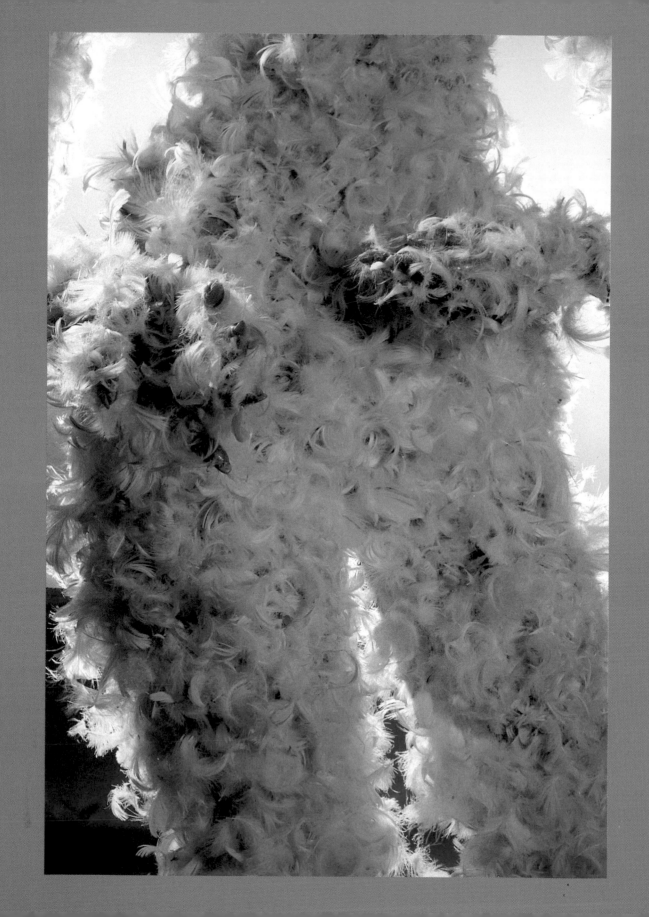

*I*N TIME, the maiden met Fitcher walking toward the house.

Now Fitcher had so many strange creatures around him that he did not remember them all, but he knew he might easily have a bird such as this one, and so he said, "Good day, Fitcher's bird—for you must have come from my house, did you not?"

"Yes," said the maiden, disguising her voice.

"Ah," said the wizard, "then can you tell me what the bride is doing?"

"I can," said the maiden. "She has prepared for the wedding and is now watching for your return."

So Fitcher walked on toward his house and saw from a distance the decorated skull in the window. Thinking it was his bride, he waved and smiled, then quickened his pace.

The maiden, meanwhile, walked on toward her father's house. On her way, she met her father and cousins and urged them to make haste.

*I*N TIME, Fitcher reached the house and went inside. While he was preparing himself for his wedding, changing his travel-stained clothes, the maiden's father and cousins arrived. They locked the doors of the house and burned it down with Fitcher in it, and so he troubled no one ever again. The three sisters lived on with their parents and, in time, all married happily and lived in joy with their husbands.

CINDY SHERMAN *was born in Glen Ridge, New Jersey, in 1954 and grew up on Long Island. She completed her undergraduate studies at New York State University College at Buffalo in 1976. During this time she was one of the founding members of the alternative gallery "Hallwalls," along with Robert Longo, Nancy Dwyer, and others. In 1977, she moved to New York City where she now lives with her husband, the French video artist Michel Auder. Numerous group and solo exhibitions in the United States, Japan, and Europe have contributed to Cindy Sherman's international fame.*

First published in the United States of America in 1992 by Rizzoli International Publications, Inc.
300 Park Avenue South, New York, New York 10010

Printed and bound by Oversea Printing Supplies, Ltd., Singapore

Design by Milton Glaser, Inc.